FASTBACK® Science Fiction

In the Zone

JON NIKISCHER

GLOBE FEARON
Pearson Learning Group

FASTBACK® SCIENCE FICTION BOOKS

The Champion	**In the Zone**
Dateline: I.P.S.	Just in Case
Eden's Daughters	Sinking Ship
The Flavorist	The Spotter
Hennesy's Test	Vital Force

Cover © Royalty-Free/Corbis. All photography © Pearson Education, Inc. (PEI) unless specifically noted.

Copyright © 2004 by Pearson Education, Inc., publishing as Globe Fearon®, an imprint of Pearson Learning Group, 299 Jefferson Road, Parsippany, NJ 07054. All rights reserved. No part of this book may be reproduced or transmitted in any form or by any means, electronic or mechanical, including photocopying, recording, or by any information storage and retrieval system, without permission in writing from the publisher. For information regarding permission(s), write to Rights and Permissions Department.

Globe Fearon® and Fastback® are registered trademarks of Globe Fearon, Inc.

ISBN 0-13-024581-X
Printed in the United States of America
1 2 3 4 5 6 7 8 9 10   07 06 05 04 03

1-800-321-3106
www.pearsonlearning.com

Eric Bronski and the other members of the cross-country track team staggered back to the locker room. Coach Washington was waiting for them. The runners shuffled past him and sat on the benches in front of their lockers. They were almost too tired to speak.

No one looked forward to what each knew was coming. They had not only lost this race; they had lost it badly. They were about to hear another long speech on the need for better training.

But the coach fooled them. "I'm not going to tell you guys you weren't ready for the race," he said. The coach stood with his back against the door. His thick arms were folded across his chest. He looked as if he thought one of them might try to escape. "You already learned that for yourselves." He paused. "And I'm not going to tell you how to train, either. I've already done that. No one listened."

Eric bent forward and took off his running shoes and socks. He began to rub his feet and his lower legs. He knew he'd have trouble walking to the showers if he didn't. Most of the guys stared at the floor, waiting for the coach to run out of steam.

Coach Washington had a disappointed look on his face. For a few moments, he didn't say anything. Then he cleared his throat. "We used to have a good track team at Kennedy High School. In fact, we used to have one of the best teams in the country."

"That was a long time ago," Eric pointed out.

"Yeah, that was when Chuck Dawes was on the team," someone else complained. "He went on to win an Olympic medal. Dawes was a champ. None of us are like him."

"Maybe one of you could be," the coach said.

That was met with a few bitter laughs but with no smiles. Eric was their best runner. He had just finished in tenth place. If there were a world-class winner among them, he was well hidden.

The coach waved them to silence. "There's someone here who wants to talk to you. After that you can get dressed and go home. I'm leaving now."

With that the coach turned and opened the door. A short, bald-headed man was waiting outside. He was a bit overweight and was old enough to be one of their fathers. And he didn't look like an athlete. But somehow he didn't seem out of place in the locker room.

"Fellas," Coach Washington said, "I'd like you to meet Chuck Dawes." Then he stepped outside and closed the door behind him.

"So this is the great Chuck Dawes," Eric thought. "He doesn't look very special."

Chuck Dawes stood where the coach had been. He seemed to be reading their minds. "I'll bet you don't think I could run a block, do you?" he asked.

"Well, maybe a block," someone said. That brought both smiles and laughter. Dawes joined in.

"It's true," Dawes said. "I haven't run a race in over ten years. But I used to be pretty good. I ran in a lot of races, and I won most of them."

Eric continued to rub his legs. "Does it ever get any easier?" he asked.

Dawes shook his head. "No, it doesn't. It gets harder."

"Then why did you do it?" someone wanted to know. "Why would anyone want to be a runner?"

Dawes shrugged. "It beats me," he said. "Some guys are good to begin with and they want to either get better or show off. I got into it before I knew how hard it was. Then, of course, it was too late."

"Why 'of course'?" Eric asked.

"Because I'm not a quitter. Once I start something, I like to finish it. I give it my best until my best isn't good enough."

"We've been doing our best," Tony Denton said from his seat near the door to the showers. "It wasn't good enough."

Chuck Dawes laughed. "Maybe you think you can fool Coach Washington. But you had better get one thing straight right now. You can't fool me. The minute I walked in here, I knew that none of you have been doing your best."

Tony pointed at his left foot. He had his sock off. A large ugly blister covered his heel. It didn't look as though Tony would be wearing shoes, let alone running, for some time. "I ran the last four miles with that," Tony said. "And you're telling me I wasn't doing my best?"

"Oh, I'm sure you all ran your hearts out today. But you haven't been doing your best. Look at you guys. You're soaked in sweat. The race has been over for 15 minutes. Some of you are still catching your breath. None of you are in shape."

Dawes ran a hand over his bald head. It was a gesture that must have been left over from the days when he had hair. "None of you were ready to run a hard race. None of you have been training as hard as you should have. You've either been missing practice or dogging it. You have to push yourselves all the time, not just during a race. If you keep pushing, you'll find you can go faster and farther each time. And you'll recover sooner, too."

"But it never gets any easier," Eric said.

"No, it doesn't. Not really. Of course, there are a few tricks."

"Tricks!" the room echoed.

Dawes rubbed his chin. "Training tricks, I mean. Things you can do to make practice more fun and less painful."

Now everyone listened closely. "Like what?" Eric asked, voicing the question in each runner's mind.

"Well," Dawes said slowly. "You might try getting in the zone."

"Huh?"

"You've got to get in the zone. I know it sounds stupid, but try to think about something else when you're practicing. Make it something as different from running as you can. Don't focus on the pain. Don't worry about how far you've gone or how many laps you still have to do. Think about swimming or football or repairing a car. Think about anything other than running."

"I guess daydreaming might not be a bad idea." Eric said.

"I'm not talking about daydreams. Daydreams are something you just fall into.

Getting in the zone is something you make happen. You force yourself to think about something else."

"Are there any other tricks?" Tony Denton asked. It was clear he wasn't buying Dawes' speech.

"Well, to get yourself started, try listening to music. It will help you get your mind off the pain. It will help you get in the zone. Soon enough, you won't need music."

"I guess it wouldn't hurt to try," Tony said.

The next afternoon, most of the team showed up with headsets. Eric Bronski brought his CD player with his favorite CD inside. Eric really didn't think this idea would work. He'd listened to music while he ran before. Still, he hadn't thought about getting in the zone before.

Eric turned on his CD player and put on the headset. He put the volume up.

At first, Eric was singing along with the music, like he'd done many times before. Between the music and the rhythmic beat of his feet hitting the track, he could feel himself getting in the zone. For no reason at all, he began to think about his last family vacation.

Last summer, his family had rented a house in the mountains. They had a great time getting away from it all. He could smell the fresh mountain air. He could hear the birds chirping. He could hear the sound of waves crashing against

10

the side of his kayak as he paddled furiously to keep up with the river's current.

Suddenly, he felt the rush of cold water soaking him as it completely covered him. The kayak had made contact with a huge wave. "Keep your wits about you," he thought to himself. "Just keep it steady."

"Oh, nooooooo!" he screamed as he saw endless waves of water feverishly washing over a group of large boulders.

He felt the bottom of the kayak hit one of the rocks and for a moment he was airborne. He landed on the raging water and was jostled forward and backward as his kayak made contact with the river. He felt the intense spray from the two-foot wave that had been determined to flip him and his kayak into the raging rapids.

"Paddle! Paddle!" he thought to himself. Then, as quickly as his adventure had started, the kayak entered a calm portion of the river. He floated peacefully between the large red rocks that surrounded him.

Before Eric knew it, practice was over! He felt like he could've kept running for hours. He had never felt so light on his feet.

"If only I'd tried this sooner," Eric thought to himself.

He remembered all the trouble he had had that year with track. He remembered how disappointed Coach Washington had been with them every time they had lost a race. He also remembered some of the advice people had given him.

"Eat pasta and bread the night before the race, and it will give you lots of energy," his father had told him. Eric did what his father suggested, but it didn't help.

Other people had advice for him, too. His mother had told him to do plenty of stretching to warm up his muscles. But he already knew that from practices with Coach Washington. His friend Becky even told him to try meditating. "It'll clear your mind so that you can concentrate in your running," she'd told him. He had followed everyone's advice, but nothing had seemed to work.

Eric took his CD player and his favorite CD to school the next day. Before track practice, he put on his CD player, hoping that it would take his mind off of running just like it had the other day. He turned up the volume and began to run.

Eric kept running. Now that he had started, he wanted to get his running practice over with.

He was in the zone. He was thinking about how much it had helped him. Then Eric noticed a flock of birds making lazy circles over the field. He looked at them and wondered what it would be like to fly.

One moment he was running around the exercise field. An instant later, he was high above it, looking down. He could see himself running laps around the track. But at the same time, he felt like a bird. *A bird!*

And he was strong. He had never thought of birds as strong, but that was how he felt now. Very strong. He thought he could fly as far and as fast as he wanted.

Eric's running had always taken a good amount of effort. Flying wasn't like that. It was as natural and as easy as breathing. And it was fun!

He made turns to the left and right. He beat his powerful wings and climbed high above the field. There he tucked his wings back and dove like an arrow. He was going so fast he thought his feathers would come off. As he neared the ground, he spread his wings to slow his flight and did a series of loops. Then he climbed again for another dive.

This time he spun wildly as he sped to the earth. He did a few more loops at the end of his plunge. It was wonderful. The sky belonged to him. The air was clean and dust-free. The sun was warm on his wings and tail feathers. Eric had never been so thrilled.

And then, as suddenly as he had left it, he was back on the track. Everyone else had stopped running. They were standing in a group and looking at the sky.

Eric jogged over to them. "What's going on?" he asked.

"Didn't you see? One of those pigeons went crazy," Bill Purdy said. "He was diving and spinning and making loops. I never saw anything like it. You must've really been in the zone to miss that.

"Yeah," said Eric. "I was in the zone, all right."

Eric walked back to where his towel was lying on the grass. He sat down. He took off his CD player and placed it in his backpack. He wiped the beads of sweat that had collected on his forehead and on the back of his neck as he thought about the adventure he had just had.

He was sure that what he had been listening to wasn't simply a CD player. It was something that had made it possible for him to become a bird for a few minutes. He didn't know if he could ever understand how it worked. And he didn't know if it would ever do it again.

His father had once told him that many of the world's greatest mysteries were never solved. They were mysteries that people had just experienced but had no explanation for. That's what made them mysteries. He said that there are some things that you can explain using science. There were other things, though, mysterious things, that could never be explained.

He took the CD player out of his backpack and turned it over and over in his hands. He opened the compartment where the CD fits and then closed it.

Could this be one of those things? Could his CD player be something mysterious? Something without explanation? How can something that I bought with money I made from my paper route be a mystery?

The more he thought about it, the

weirder he felt. Maybe the rechargeable batteries he'd bought were making his CD player act funny. He knew one thing, though. His CD player made being in the zone strange and fun all at the same time.

Did it work only with animals, or could he change places with a person? Would being in the zone let him go back to the past? Into the future? What were the limits? *Were* there any limits?

The most important question was whether it would work again.

Eric put on his CD player and turned it on. He looked around. Coach Washington had come out of the school building.

"I wonder what it would be like to be Coach Washington," Eric thought.

And then he was. He was Coach Washington, standing by the door to the gym and looking out at the practice field.

He saw himself, Eric, sitting on the grass. He saw the other members of the track team at different points on the field. He felt pleased. He thought to himself:

"Everyone has shown up for practice. Whatever Chuck Dawes said must have worked. It's too bad about my timing, though. I know the guys can't get into shape soon enough to turn the season around. This may be my last year as coach. The school might look for someone who can get the team fired up quicker than I can.

"There's Bill Purdy standing at the edge of the track. He's watching the birds. It's just like him. It takes very little to keep him from working out. But from the look of his gym shirt, he's already done some running. Even Tony Denton, the boy who hurt his foot, has turned up. He's wisely sitting on the bleachers near the baseball diamond, not trying to run. And Eric Bronski seems to have finished practice already. That's good. He could become a fine runner if only he'd work a little harder. He's got the small compact frame all the really good distance runners seem to have. All legs and lungs, as I like to say. With two years of hard work, he—"

In the next moment, Eric was back sitting on the grass. Across the field he could see Coach Washington shaking his head as though to clear it. The coach looked over the field one more time and went inside.

Eric hadn't known the coach was worried about his job. It was a fear he had kept from the team.

Eric didn't think he should tell a secret he learned while he was in the zone. But everyone liked the coach and would hate to lose him. He was tough, but he was always fair. Who knew what a new coach would be like?

If anything would give the team a reason to work hard, this was it. Before he left the field, Eric told everyone the coach's job might depend on how well they did in the next few races. Then he took a shower and went home.

Eric had trouble getting to sleep that night. He couldn't take his mind off his CD player. He thought about how it had helped him get in the zone and about how much more comfortable running had become. "This is a mystery if I ever heard of one," he thought.

But he still had no idea how it worked. The only way to find out very much would be to take it apart. But he didn't dare do that. What if he couldn't get it back together the same way? What if he broke it? Rather than chance making a mistake, he decided to do nothing. That seemed the only safe course to take. Eric didn't want anything to keep him from being able to get in the zone.

The next day, two of his teachers caught him daydreaming. They had called on him to answer questions, but his mind had been somewhere else. He was thinking about what he might try to do next with his CD player.

When it was time to go out to the track after class, Eric still hadn't made up his mind. Knowing what it was like to walk on the moon would be interesting. So would commanding a submarine. It was hard to choose. Eric figured he'd do both. He put on his CD player and went outside.

Coach Washington spoiled his plans before Eric could decide what to do first. The coach was waiting near the track when the team came out of the locker room. His stopwatch was hanging from a cord around his neck.

"I'm going to clock you guys today," he said. "Let's see how your time for ten kilometers compares with what you did six weeks ago." He pointed to the starting blocks. "Line up and let's make a race of it."

One time around the track was 250 meters. Four laps equaled 1000. Forty laps were therefore ten kilometers. The race was only about six miles. Eric had been planning to run ten miles. But he hadn't intended to push himself. With the coach standing by with his stopwatch, it promised to be a hard six miles.

Eric lined up with the rest of the team. He placed himself between Bill Purdy and long-legged Spider O'Dale. The coach fired his starting gun, and the runners took off.

The last time the coach had clocked him, Eric's time hadn't been very good. Eric had no reason to think it would be any better today. He hoped it would be, though, if only to make the coach feel better.

At the end of the first lap, Eric was out in front. He set the team's pace. As he passed the spot where Coach Washington stood, Eric glanced at the man. The coach was looking down at the stopwatch. He had an unhappy look on his face.

Chuck Dawes had been one of the coach's runners. Dawes had held records in every distance race from 10,000 meters to the marathon. Because the coach had worked with Dawes, it was no wonder he expected so much from his teams. He'd had the best. He would never be pleased with less.

Dawes had won his Olympic medal in the 10,000-meter run. It must have been quite a race. Eric wondered what it would be like to run in the Olympics and win a medal. "Wait a minute!" he said to himself. "Why didn't I think of this before?"

Eric was on the far side of the track. He reached up and clicked on his radio. He carefully worded the thought "I wonder what it was like to be Chuck Dawes in the Olympics?"

Nothing happened. Eric was still pounding along on the track. But then he noticed that it *wasn't* the same track. It was in better shape. The high school's track had a few ruts in it. This one was smooth and well graded. Eric glanced back over his shoulder at the other runners. He didn't recognize any of them. Purdy, O'Dale, and his other buddies had been replaced by strangers. The strangers seemed determined to run Eric into the ground.

He picked up his pace. He knew just how fast he was going. He knew how far he had already run and how far he still had to go. His arms swung in rhythm with his strides as he flashed over the ground. He felt strong and sure of himself. His breathing wasn't labored; there was no strain in his movements. Only being in the zone as a bird could compare to this.

After Eric had covered 6,000 meters, he heard the faint footfall of someone coming up behind him. His lead was being challenged. Eric increased his speed until the man dropped back. Then he returned to his normal ground-eating pace. After the short sprint, it was almost like coasting.

All of Eric's attention had been on the track. He hadn't noticed the crowd in the stands. The crowd watched in silence until there were only two laps to go. Then it began shouting and cheering the runners on. Eric knew that some of the shouts were being directed at him. It made him feel good. He leaned forward and lengthened his strides.

Eric knew he was going to win this race. But he wanted to do more than that. He wanted to break the world's record when he did it.

And then the ruts were back in the track.

And the other runners were about 50 yards ahead of him. They no longer trailed far behind him.

The cheering from the stands had stopped.

Coach Washington was staring at Eric in shock. It was no wonder. Eric was supposed to be his best runner. Here he was plodding along in last place.

Eric put his mind back in gear and ran as hard as he could. He wanted at least to catch up before the race was over.

He was still several yards behind the pack when it crossed the finish line.

Everyone turned to him in disbelief. Eric couldn't look anyone in the eye. He hung his head. He felt so ashamed. He had never finished a race in last place. Never.

No one said a word.

Finally, Coach Washington came over to Eric and said, "That was some race you ran."

"Yeah," Eric replied. What else could he say?

"I always thought you had the makings of a runner."

"You're the only one who did," Eric said.

"Would you like to take a look at your time?" The coach held out his stopwatch.

Eric glanced at it, turned away, and then looked quickly back at the watch. "Hey! That says—"

"It says you were a couple of seconds off the high school record," the coach broke in, his face split by a broad smile. "You almost passed everyone on the extra lap you ran."

Passed them? Then he wasn't behind. He was so far ahead that he had run an extra lap. That's why he was getting the strange looks.

"I had a good day," Eric said.

"And you'll have more of them," the coach predicted.

"Yes, I guess I will," Eric said. No matter where his mind had been during the race, it was his body that had done the running. When he had been in the zone as a bird, he hadn't actually flown. He hadn't become a bird. But he *was* a runner. And he had just run faster than he'd ever thought he could.

He had a lot to learn about himself.

The days, weeks, months, and years ahead were going to be filled with discovery and adventure.